7/13

Fact Finders®

The Story of the
American Revolution

Heroes
of the
American Revolution

by Mary Hertz Scarbrough

Consultant:
Richard Bell
Assistant Professor, Department of History
University of Maryland
College Park, Maryland

CAPSTONE PRESS
a capstone imprint

Fact Finders are published by Capstone Press,
1710 Roe Crest Drive, North Mankato, Minnesota 56003.
www.capstonepub.com

Library of Congress Cataloging-in-Publication Data
Scarbrough, Mary Hertz.
Heroes of the American Revolution / by Mary Hertz Scarbrough.
p. cm. — (Fact finders—the story of the American Revolution)
Includes bibliographical references and index.
Summary: "Describes notable heroes of the American Revolution"—Provided
by publisher.
ISBN 978-1-4296-8590-0 (library binding)
ISBN 978-1-4296-9286-1 (paperback)
ISBN 978-1-62065-246-6 (ebook PDF)
1. United States—History—Revolution, 1775–1783—Juvenile literature.
2. United States—History—Revolution, 1775–1783—Biography—Juvenile literature.
I. Title.

E208.S297 2013
973.3092'2—dc23
[B]   2011048657

Editorial Credits
Mari Bolte, editor; Heidi Thompson, designer; Wanda Winch, media researcher;
Laura Manthe, production specialist

Photo Credits
Alamy: North Wind Picture Archives, 9, 11, 26, 29; Corbis: Bettmann, 10, 24; Getty
Images Inc: National Geographic/Louis S. Glanzman, 13; Library of Congress: Prints
and Photographs Division, 12, 15, 16, 17, 21, 28; National Archives and Records
Administration: 14, 19; Newscom: Picture History, 18; rickreevesstudio.com: Rick Reeves,
23; Shutterstock: Christophe Boisson, grunge background; SuperStock Inc: SuperStock, 5

Printed in the United States of America in Stevens Point, Wisconsin.
022013   007180R

Table of Contents

Direct quotations appear on the following pages:

Page 12, from *Common Sense*, by Thomas Paine (Philadelphia: W. and T. Bradford, 1776.)

Page 21, from *Lafayette in the Age of the American Revolution: Selected Letters and Papers, 1776–1790*, ed. by Stanley J. Idzerda (Ithaca, N.Y.: Cornell University Press, 1977.)

CHAPTER 1

Unrest in the Colonies

The American Revolution (1775–1783) was a war of rebellion. Before the war, Great Britain controlled the 13 colonies. The colonists fought this control. Some people fought with weapons, while others fought with words. Heroes stepped forward. Colonists wrote or spoke out against British rule in public. They organized protests against Great Britain. They put their lives on the line serving in the Continental army.

The war started over debt and who should pay it. The recent French and Indian War (1754–1763) had been expensive for Great Britain. The country needed a lot of money that it didn't have. The British government decided to get some of the money by taxing its subjects, including the colonists.

Colonists thought the taxes were unfair. Some people refused to pay or boycotted the taxed items.

colonist: someone who lives in a newly settled area

tax: money collected from a country's citizens to help pay for running the government

boycott: to refuse to take part in something as a way of making a protest

The colonists were upset that the taxes had been placed on them without their consent.

Many colonists were simply unhappy with the way they were ruled. They were subjects of the British government and had to pay British taxes. But they had no say in how the government was run.

Many men and women of the colonies were ready to make a stand. These heroes made their actions felt and their voices heard. The war against Great Britain was just beginning.

Timeline of the American Revolution

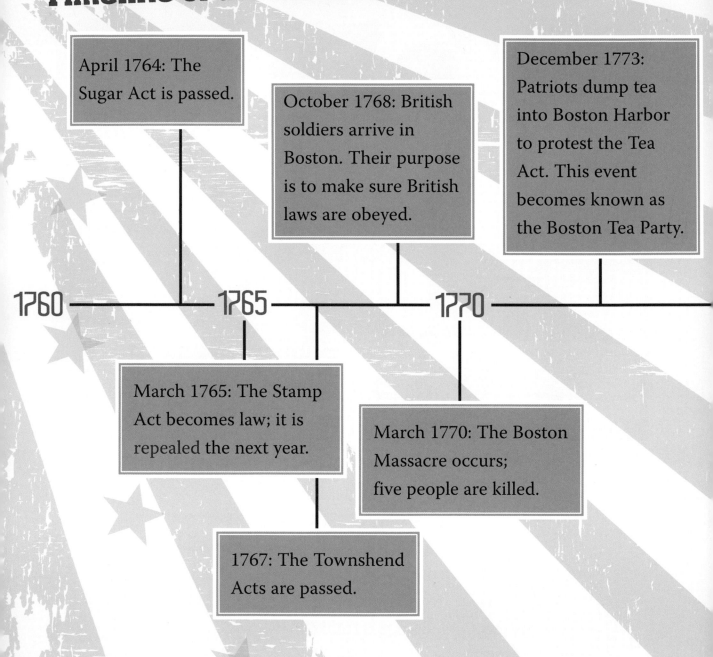

April 1764: The Sugar Act is passed.

October 1768: British soldiers arrive in Boston. Their purpose is to make sure British laws are obeyed.

December 1773: Patriots dump tea into Boston Harbor to protest the Tea Act. This event becomes known as the Boston Tea Party.

1760

1765

1770

March 1765: The Stamp Act becomes law; it is repealed the next year.

March 1770: The Boston Massacre occurs; five people are killed.

1767: The Townshend Acts are passed.

repeal: to officially cancel something, such as a law

April 1775: First shots of the war are fired at Lexington and Concord.

September–October 1781: Battle of Yorktown; the last major battle of the Revolutionary War.

December 1776: Benjamin Franklin convinces France to help in the war effort.

July 1777: Battle of Fort Ticonderoga; British victory.

1775

1780

1785

September 1783: The United States and Great Britain sign a peace treaty, officially ending the war.

June 1775: Battle of Bunker Hill; neither side wins.

September 1774: The First Continental Congress meets.

October 1777: Battle of Saratoga; Patriot victory.

July 4, 1776: The Continental Congress approves the Declaration of Independence.

CHAPTER 2

Heroes with Words

In September 1774, 56 men from across the colonies met in Philadelphia, Pennsylvania, for the First Continental Congress. The people who attended the meeting included lawyers, politicians, and military leaders. Most of the attendees wanted to ease the tensions between Great Britain and the colonies. At the time, independence was not something they seriously considered.

The men sent a Declaration of Rights to Great Britain's King George III. Colonists hoped the king would listen and remove the taxes. But colonial leaders planned to meet the following year if the situation didn't improve.

The king and the British Parliament didn't back down. In 1775 the British government moved in to take weapons the colonists had stored in Massachusetts. The Patriots rode out to meet the British soldiers. Suddenly, a shot rang out. No one knows who fired the shot, but the British soldiers opened fire in response.

parliament: a group of people who make laws and run the government in some countries

The colonists now saw that war was their only option. Heroic leaders in the colonies stepped forward to take charge. They used their words to encourage their fellow colonists to stand for independence.

Eight colonists were killed in what would be called the Battles of Lexington and Concord.

Patrick Henry

Patrick Henry was an outspoken Patriot. He was a popular lawyer and politician. Henry believed the colonies needed to raise an army. In 1775 he spoke out to convince the people of Virginia to fight against the British. Henry rallied the leaders of Virginia by stating, "Give me liberty, or give me death!" Although no one recorded his words as he spoke, they are still remembered today.

Patrick Henry led the colonial rebellion against the Stamp Act of 1765.

Samuel Adams

Samuel Adams wasn't surprised by the king's response to the Declaration of Rights. Adams, a politician and former tax collector, had been speaking out against Great Britain since the 1760s. He wrote attacks against the British in Boston's newspapers. His letters called for the colonists to resist British rule. He led protests against the Stamp and Sugar Acts.

Adams founded the Sons of Liberty in 1765. He was also one of the men behind the Boston Tea Party in 1773. He was the first to propose a Continental Congress and served as a representative when the congress met. In 1776 he was one of the first to sign the Declaration of Independence.

In Great Britain, Samuel Adams (left) was known as "the most dangerous man in Massachusetts."

Thomas Paine

Thomas Paine didn't come to the colonies until 1774. But he was inspired by the Patriots' fight for freedom. He called it a "new era in politics." Paine was a talented writer who used words wisely. His pamphlet, *Common Sense*, was printed in early 1776.

Paine's 46-page booklet stated that war was the only sensible answer to the conflict between Britain and the colonies. He wrote that it was foolish for a big piece of land like North America to be controlled by a tiny island.

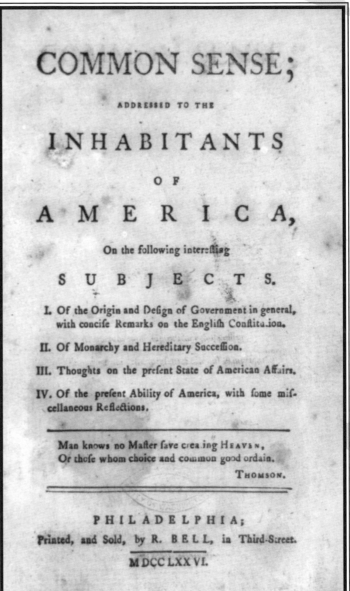

Paine gave the profits from the sale of *Common Sense* to the Continental army.

... There is something very absurd, in supposing a continent to be perpetually governed by an island. ... it is evident they belong to different systems: England to Europe, America to itself.

—Thomas Paine, *Common Sense*

Paine wrote other radical pamphlets. In 1791 he supported the French Revolution by writing *The Rights of Man*. He was arrested by the French government in 1793 but released the following year.

Paine also wrote that the king's role was meaningless to the colonists. He felt it would be easy for the colonists to defeat the British. *Common Sense* was an instant bestseller and sold thousands of copies in its first year. George Washington would use Paine's words to inspire discouraged soldiers.

Thomas Jefferson

Common Sense set the spark of independence. Thomas Jefferson turned those sparks into flames. He wasn't afraid to question British laws.

In May 1775 the Second Continental Congress met. Everyone agreed the time to fight for independence had come. The colonies would begin printing paper money later that year.

The men chosen to draft the Declaration of Independence were Benjamin Franklin, Thomas Jefferson, John Adams, Robert Livingston, and Roger Sherman.

And they would have their own army.

Five men, including Jefferson, were chosen to draft the Declaration of Independence. The document would tell the world why America needed to be its own country. Jefferson was the main author, but notes and comments were added by the others. The Declaration of Independence was adopted and signed on July 4, 1776.

Benjamin Franklin

Benjamin Franklin had been elected to represent the colonies in Great Britain. He spent 15 years in London. At first he thought obeying Parliament would be best for everyone. However, after seeing how Great Britain treated the colonists, Franklin changed his mind.

In 1766 Franklin asked Parliament to repeal the taxes on the colonies. The taxes were reversed, but new taxes were set the following year. Franklin returned home in 1774.

In 1776 Franklin accepted the title of Minister to France. He traveled to Paris to convince the French to support the colonists' cause. The French idolized Franklin and gave him money to help the colonies. Frenchmen began traveling to the colonies to offer their support. On April 30, 1778, France officially entered the war.

FAST FACTS

During the war, letter writers signed their names in the top corner of the letter's envelope. Franklin signed his letters "B. Free Franklin" as a protest against British rule.

Battlefield Heroes

Many heroes took a stand against Great Britain on the battlefield. But they fought more than just British soldiers. Weapons were deadly and disease spread quickly. More than 100,000 soldiers would lose their lives during the American Revolution. Without the heroes who led the colonial army, the war would have been lost.

George Washington

George Washington enlisted in the Virginia militia in 1752. In 1758 he entered politics. He helped make decisions about the colonies and spoke at the Continental Congress. In 1775 he was chosen to lead the Continental army.

In October 1775, the Continental Congress approved Washington's request for an army of 20,732 men.

Washington was told to expect about 17,000 militiamen. He found himself nearly 6,000 soldiers short. Stragglers arrived at their leisure, making it difficult for everyone to train at once. It seemed impossible that this ragtag militia of enlisted men would be able to defeat the British army.

Local militias had their own weapons, uniforms, and drills. This made training the militias together difficult.

The militiamen knew they were at a disadvantage in battle. Many fled when they spotted British officers. Washington decided to fight defensively. The British would have to spend most of their time chasing or tracking down the militia. Then Washington would launch a surprise attack.

enlist: to voluntarily join a branch of the military

militia: a group of citizens who are trained to fight, but who only serve in an emergency

17

Henry Knox

Washington's army would not have been successful without loyal officers. In 1775 Washington was ready to attack the British in Boston. But his men were short on weapons. The army had recently captured some artillery, but the weapons were about 300 miles (483 kilometers) away. Artillery commander Henry Knox took charge of collecting them. He towed the weapons across ice and over rough, hilly land. Over a six-week period, Knox picked up

Knox transported the artillery using 40 sleds pulled by 80 teams of oxen.

60 tons (54 metric tons) of artillery, including 59 big guns.

Knox's cannons arrived in March 1776. They were moved to a position overlooking Boston. The British left Boston soon after.

artillery: cannons and other large guns used during battles

Nathanael Greene

In 1780 Washington put Major General Nathanael Greene in charge of the army in the southern colonies. The southern army had a history of poor leaders. They had suffered so many losses that the Patriots were no longer a threat in the south. Greene adopted Washington's defensive fighting style with great success. Under Greene, the army won the lost territories and captured many British prisoners of war.

Nathanael Greene was one of the only colonial officers to serve throughout the American Revolution.

Two Fighting Forces

The colonists had two separate forces—the militia and the Minutemen. The colonial militia was formed in the late 1600s. It was made up of volunteers between the ages of 16 and 60. They held training days to practice their skills.

The Minutemen were elite members of the militia. They had trained heavily in the 16 months between the Boston Tea Party and the Battles of Lexington and Concord. They were expected to be battle-ready in 60 seconds.

The Continental army was created by the Second Continental Congress in 1775. Militiamen agreed to fight in the army for one to three years in return for payment.

CHAPTER 4

Heroes from Other Lands

Even with brave fighters on the home front, the colonists needed help to win the war. Men from other lands helped ensure the colonists' victory. Without the help of the foreign officers who traveled to the colonies, the war may have been lost.

Marquis de Lafayette

The 19-year-old Marquis de Lafayette arrived in America in 1777 from France. Although he was young and rich, he was an experienced fighter.

Lafayette was impressed by the colonists' dedication to their cause. He refused a salary and lived in the same poor conditions as his soldiers. He used his personal riches to buy his men guns and uniforms. The men called him "the soldier's friend." Lafayette and his men aided Washington during the final attack at Yorktown. The additional soldiers gave the Continentals the numbers they needed to win the war.

marquis: a European nobleman

This devil Cornwallis ... inspires me with a sincere fear, and his name has greatly troubled my sleep. This campaign is a good school for me. God grant that the public does not pay for my lessons.

—Marquis de Lafayette, July 9, 1781

George Washington and his officers. From left, Washington, Johann De Kalb, Baron von Steuben, Kazimierz Pulaski, Thaddeus Kosciuszko, Marquis de Lafayette, John Muhlenberg.

Thaddeus Kosciuszko

Polish engineer Thaddeus Kosciuszko arrived in America in 1776. His job was to fortify battlegrounds by reinforcing the area with available materials, such as logs, ditches, or mounds of earth. In 1777 he was sent to Fort Ticonderoga in New York. However, his defensive advice was ignored. When the British attacked, the fort fell.

As the Continental army fled, Kosciuszko flooded streams, cut down trees, and destroyed bridges. His actions slowed the British soldiers' pursuit, giving the colonists time to plan their next attack site. They chose an area near Saratoga, New York. Kosciuszko's defenses made it nearly impossible for the British to successfully attack. The Americans won the Battle of Saratoga, a major turning point in the war.

Baron von Steuben

Prussian Baron von Steuben reached the colonies in February 1778. He would teach the troops to fight. The British soldiers were highly disciplined and experienced. In comparison, the Continental army was made up of many state militias. Each militia had its own rules, and all were poorly trained.

First, von Steuben advised the officers to win their soldiers' trust. They should also put the mens' needs first.

fortify: to construct walls or buildings to be used as military defenses

Von Steuben wrote a manual of his military drills. The book was the U.S. military's training guide until 1812.

Then von Stueben put the officers in charge of drills. Previously, drilling the soldiers was a job for sergeants. But in battle, the officers gave the commands. Having the officers drill with the men ensured that commands would be understood during battle. With von Steuben's help, the Continental army had a fighting chance.

Later that year, King Louis XVI of France sent 5,500 soldiers to the colonies. The extra soldiers were enough to help the colonists win the Battle of Yorktown in 1781. This battle victory led to British General Lord Charles Cornwallis' surrender. His defeat led to the end of the Revolutionary War.

CHAPTER 5

America's First Spies

Spies used both words and weapons to fight during the war. They crossed enemy lines to gather important information and pass messages to aid their cause.

Nancy Morgan Hart

Nancy Morgan Hart was one of those spies. She gathered information on the British army. She was also determined to rid Georgia of British Loyalists.

Hart (right) was known for her skills with a gun. The local Cherokee people called her "War Woman."

One evening, six British soldiers rode to the Hart house and demanded to be fed. As they dined, Hart told her daughter to alert the Continental army. Then Hart stole the soldiers' weapons. When the soldiers noticed what was happening, Hart pointed one of the guns at them. She was able to hold them until the Continentals arrived. The soldiers were executed.

Nathan Hale

Former schoolteacher Nathan Hale was one of America's first spies. He was sent to spy on British army camps.

Hale's commanding officer knew nothing about spying. He sent Hale across enemy lines without any spy training or tools. Hale was soon discovered. When questioned by the British, his accent and posture gave him away. He was also found hiding documents that proved he was a spy.

Hale was killed at the age of 21. He was the first American executed as a spy. Before his execution, he reportedly said, **"I only regret that I have but one life to lose for my country."**

By admitting he was a Patriot soldier, Hale sealed his fate.

Hale's death made it clear that the Patriots needed a better spy system. At George Washington's request, colonial Major Benjamin Tallmadge recruited about 20 people to form the Culper Ring. The ring was a secret intelligence agency that specialized in the New York City area.

The group was extremely secret. Not even Washington knew who all the members were. To prevent their messages from being discovered, they used invisible ink and secret codes. They passed valuable information on to Washington over a two-year period.

Tools of the Trade

Spies used many tricks to gain information. Invisible ink could send coded messages across enemy lines. A good spy system could ensure messages would be passed quickly and quietly.

Sometimes all it took was a good disguise. According to legend, Nancy Morgan Hart would pretend to be mentally ill. She was able to walk right into British camps.

Invisible ink was made from a chemical called ferrous sulfate mixed with water. The ink would appear when the paper was held over heat or brushed with another substance. To make reading even more difficult, the message was written between the lines of books or pamphlets.

Messages could also be sent by code. One code assigned certain words and names a number between 1 and 763. For example, "Washington" was 711, and "attack" was 38.

recruit: to ask someone to join a company or organization

James Armistead

James Armistead was a slave who had joined the Continental army with his master's permission. He served under the Marquis de Lafayette. He also spied on the British army by pretending to be an escaped slave. He was able to convince the British that he was spying on the Continentals. Eventually he gained the trust of British Generals Charles Cornwallis and Benedict Arnold.

Armistead gathered valuable information. Eventually he learned that Cornwallis was moving his soldiers to Yorktown, Virginia. The Continental army trapped Cornwallis in Yorktown and forced his surrender.

The Marquis de Lafayette (left) and a man believed to be Armistead. After the war, the Marquis helped Armistead gain his freedom. The newly-freed Armistead chose "Lafayette" as his last name, in honor of the general.

The British surrendered after the Battle of Yorktown in 1781.

There were many heroes of the Revolutionary War. The strong colonial leaders inspired their men to fight. Foreign officers brought soldiers and knowledge, which they shared with the colonists. Spies behind enemy lines risked their life for liberty. Without these heroes, the Revolutionary War might never have been won.

Glossary

artillery (ar-TI-luhr-ee)—cannons and other large guns used during battles

boycott (BOY-kot)—to refuse to take part in something as a way of making a protest

colonist (KAH-luh-nist)—someone who lives in a newly settled area

enlist (en-LIST)—to voluntarily join a branch of the military

fortify (FOR-tuh-fye)—to make a place stronger against attack

marquis (mar-KEE)—a European nobleman

militia (muh-LISH-uh)—a group of citizens who are trained to fight, but who only serve in an emergency

parliament (PAR-luh-muhnt)—a group of people who make laws and run the government in some countries

recruit (ri-KROOT)—to ask someone to join a company or organization

repeal (ri-PEEL)—to officially cancel something, such as a law

tax (TAKS)—money collected from a country's citizens to help pay for running the government

Read More

Burgan, Michael. *Weapons, Gear, and Uniforms of the American Revolution.* Equipped for Battle. Mankato, Minn.: Capstone Press, 2012.

Gregory, Josh. *The Revolutionary War.* Cornerstones of Freedom. New York: Children's Press, 2012.

Samuels, Charlie. *Timeline of the Revolutionary War.* Americans at War. New York: Gareth Stevens Pub., 2012.

Internet Sites

FactHound offers a safe, fun way to find Internet sites related to this book. All of the sites on FactHound have been researched by our staff.

Here's all you do:

Visit *www.facthound.com*

Type in this code: 9781429685900

Super-cool stuff! Check out projects, games and lots more at www.capstonekids.com

Index